Paul Biya: The Living Specter that is Haunting the Cameroonian People

Janvier Tchouteu

TISI BOOKS

NEW YORK, RALEIGH, LONDON, AMSTERDAM

PUBLISHED BY TISI BOOKS

www.tisibooks.com

ISBN-13: 978-1-7179-9638-1

ISBN-10: 1-7179-9638-8

PUBLISHED BY TISI BOOKS

www.tisibooks.com

NEW YORK, RALEIGH, LONDON, AMSTERDAM

Printed in The United States of America

Titles by Janvier Chouteu-Chando

The Usurper: and Other Stories
Triple Agent, Double Cross
Disciples of Fortune
The Union Moujik
Splendid Comets
Flash of the Sun
Fortune Calls
Fortune's Master
Fortune's Children
The Norilsk Bears
To Be In Love and To Be Wise
The Fire and Ice Legend
The Sweetest Madness
The Grandmothers
The Hunger Fire
The Shades of Fire
Father and Sons
The Doctors
Dark Shades
Fateful Ties
The Verdict of Hades
His Majesty's Trial
Ngoko's Folly
The Usurper
The Dowry
I am Hated
The Oaf

Non-Fiction Titles by Janvier Chouteu-Chando

FALLEN HEROES: African Leaders Whose Assassinations…
BROKEN ENGAGEMENT: Why a Donald Trump Win…
THEIR LAST STAND: Donald Trump's Upset Victory…
Ukraine: The Tug-of-war between Russia and the West
THE CANARY IN A COAL MINE EFFECT:…
Cameroon: The Haunted Heart of Africa

Quotes

You see these dictators on their pedestals, surrounded by the bayonets of their soldiers and the truncheons of their police ... yet in their hearts there is unspoken fear. They are afraid of words and thoughts: words spoken abroad, thoughts stirring at home --- all the more powerful because forbidden --- terrify them. A little mouse of thought appears in the room, and even the mightiest potentates are thrown into panic.

Winston Churchill

"If we fight to the death against an arbitrary integration of our country into the French colonial empire, it is because we want to remain the conquering defenders of the right of peoples to self-determination. We are thus, in the service of Kamerun and Africa...we are the true craftsmen of international detente. As revolutionary nationalists, we are fighting to realize for the Kamerun and for it alone, a true national "Independence" with "Unification" as a precondition, simultaneous or consecutive, but never excluded."

Ruben Um Nyobè

"Without Africa, France will have no history in the 21st century."

François Mitterrand, 1957

"We are not involved in this struggle only because we think that we will dismantle this system in the course of our life. We hope Cameroon changes tomorrow. But if it doesn't, we will be happy to know that we made the ground fertile for the next generation that will end the rot in this country, and then establish the "NEW CAMEROON"."
Dr. Samuel F. Tchwenko, former UPCist and chief ideologue of the historic SDF of 1990-2002

"Until the lions have their own historians, the history of the hunt will always glorify the hunter."
Chinua Achebe

"Cameroon is not a country of slaves that no man can free."
Janvier Chouteu-Chando

"To be sure, dictators are crafty, evil geniuses with awesome firepower at their disposal. They are also brutally efficient at intimidation, terrorism, and mass slaughter. However, a force is able to dominate because the counterforce is either nonexistent or weak.
George B.N Ayittey

"...The world gets blessed every now and then with unique souls who though burdened by their invisible crosses, still have the extraordinary strength to forge ahead in life and give others a helping hand at the same time. Despite their tribulations, most of us think they are fine. Even when the weight of their crosses become unbearable, even when they proceed in a breathless manner, we still have a hard time understanding that they are drowning. In fact, we even condemn them for failing to sacrifice more..."
Janvier Chouteu-Chando, Disciples of Fortune

"Africa is my country and Cameroon my family."
Didier Banlock

"The use of political assassination against liberation movements has changed the course of history in a number of countries in Africa and continues to devastate the Middle East. The current power relations between the Third World and the dominant Western and imperialist powers, are a product of the war of attrition which the West has waged, particularly by political assassinations, which have robbed Africa and the Middle East of some of their great leaders, and weakened their important political organizations."
— Victoria Brittain

Contents

EPIGRAPH

"The time for revolutionaries with total freedom to maneuver is over."
CHRISTOPHER KWAYEP-CHANDO

DEDICATION

This book is dedicated to the loving memory of Solomon Tandeng Muna Yakana.

ACKNOWLEDGMENTS

My deepest, warmest and everlasting thanks to Dr. Samuel F. Tchwenko and Christopher N. Chando for their contributions in chiseling the national idea for the "New Cameroon".

Maps

African Democracy Ratings

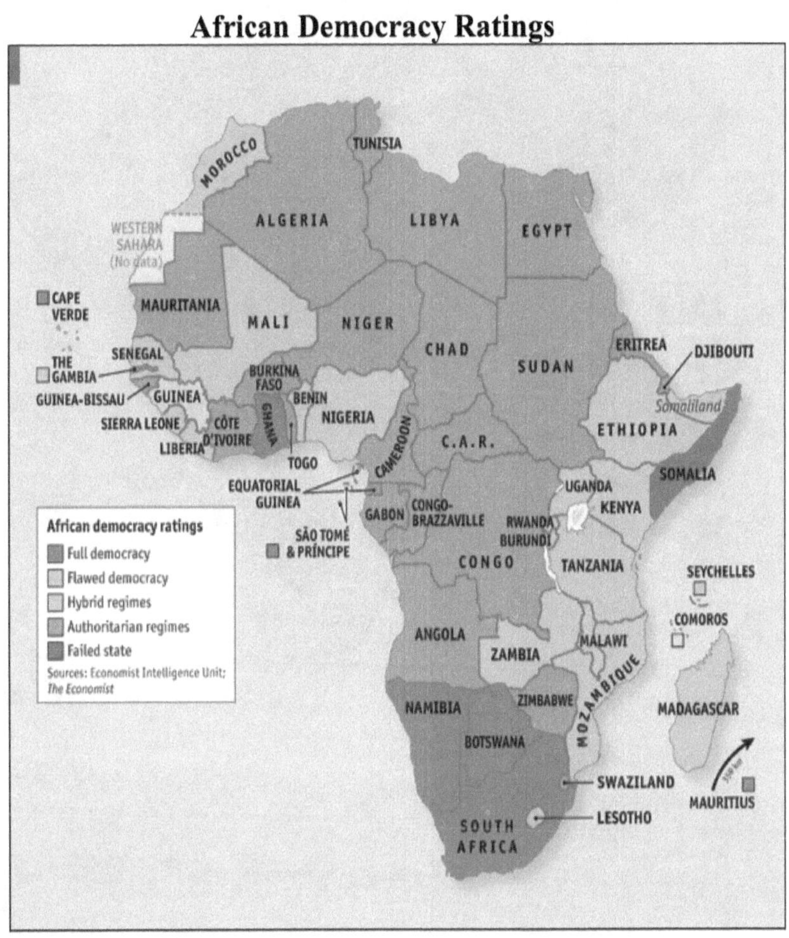

Partition Map of Africa: 1884-1914

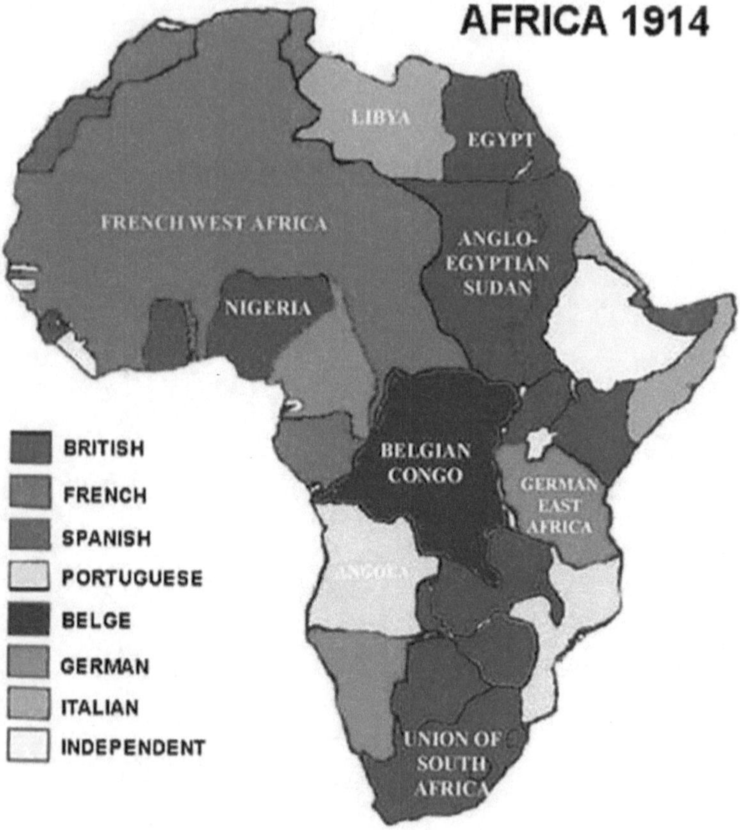

Cameroon on a map of the world

Cameroon over time

1. German Kamerun I (1884-1911)
2. German Kamerun II (1911-1916)
3. British Cameroons&French Cameroun: 1916-1960
4. British Cameroons&La Republique du Cameroun (1960-1961)
5. British Southern Cameroons&La Republique du Cameroun (1960-1961)
6. Reunited/Independent Cameroon today.

Paul Biya: The Living Specter that is Haunting the Cameroonian People

Introduction

Cameroon's unfinished liberation struggle is into its fourth phase already, having suffered defeat in the hands of its former colonial masters led by France, and the puppets France put in power before granting French Cameroun independence on January 01, 1960.

The Cameroonian patriots languished in defeat, but they never gave up the struggle. Today, a new generation of Cameroonian patriots variously described as the Kamerunists, union-nationalists and Cameroonian civic-nationalists picked up the baton dropped by the leaders of the country's historic UPC (Union of the Populations of the Cameroons) of 1948-1971, and the later generation civic-nationalists who joined the SDF (Social Democratic Front) in 190-1991 believing that its leadership was committed to the struggle to complete the liberation of Cameroon. The advocates of change in these post-independence generations, who are not compromised by the anachronistic French-imposed system, oppose not only the 34-year regime of Cameroon's current head of state Paul Biya, but also the foundations of the system that Gaullist France put in place before handing power to Paul Biya's predecessor Ahmadou Ahidjo.

In these accounts, we are presented with a struggle that is not blinded by emotions, a struggle that is grounded on humanitarianism and social solidarity, a struggle that holds no rancor against the French people but reject that fringe of the French political establishment, a political mafia per se, that is controlling Francophone Africa (FrancAfrique) and that sustains the Cameroonian dictatorship against the choice and wishes of the Cameroonian people.

CHAPTER ONE

PAUL BIYA, THE HEAD OF STATE OF CAMEROON:
The Living Specter that is Haunting Cameroonians

Pose this question to any Cameroonian with a deep perception of the world: Who is Africa's most dishonest and illusionary head of state? The answer from the absolute majority would be obvious. Our tenant in the unity palace is that head of state.

Cameroon's second president is a bad leader in the furthest sense of the word. His governance has destroyed most of the foundations of our people's way of life and progressive values. Unprincipled, unscrupulous and visionless, he was elusive enough during his early years of leadership by convincing many to regard him as a brilliant leader. Yes, he made himself brilliant and appealing to the people even despite his true convictions.

The second Cameroonian president as the demagogue he is, harangued about his NEW DEAL of Rigor and Moralization, when he never intended to work for the interest of all Cameroonians. He came to power for the sole purpose of defending the interest of his patron(The mafia in the French establishment over its African policy), to enhance the material well-being and social position of his clique of unscrupulous businessmen, politicians, functionaries and above all the ethnic group of his birth.

A second Cameroonian president is a dishonorable man without convictions. He began his political manifestations as a Cameroonian nationalist of socialist orientation under the banner of the Union of the Populations of Cameroon (UPC), but soon unhesitatingly discarded his nationalist garment for the high positions offered to renegades of the Cameroonian struggle by the Anglophobic Ahidjo regime and its French masters. Having switched his loyalty to the glory of naked power in the French-backed regime overseeing the genocide of the union-nationalist forces in Cameroon, Paul Biya quickly won the hearts of his patron to become prime minister in 1972 and later president in 1982. After that, he shed all aspects of his ties to Cameroonian nationalism and became a fervent Francophile and Anglophone manipulator. Today, it is clear for all to see that Paul Biya stands as the leader of the renegade forces that may eventually kill Cameroonian nationalism and lead the nation into the abyss, denying it the realization of its century-old Cameroonian dream of unity, independence, prosperity and open opportunities. He is a purposeless, faceless and paranoiac leader whose long years of power and the emptiness of his rule have been masked by France and his Cameroonian collaborators.

During his early years as head of state, Paul Biya talked of rigor in the implementation of progressive work ethics, rules, laws, freedom, Human rights and economic reforms, when he never intended to see the slightest change in the

French imposed system he inherited from his predecessor. Biya never had any intention to change the course of dictatorship, corruption, kleptomania, and division that was the rule of the system and the trappings of power and wealth it offered. A decade after his pronouncement of rigor, Cameroon which had the second fastest economic growth rate in the world after South Korea in 1986(though it lagged behind its true potentials even then), is today with the least promising economy in Africa.

Biya's moralization rhetoric is an unacceptable abuse to humanity. Promising to make his rule a moral one where governance would be based on a program to enhance the right conducts in public, social, economic and political affairs, he reneged by presiding over the worst degeneration of a non-war ravaged nation in Africa.

Unfortunately, for Cameroonians, Biya is one of those regrettable products of nature with quite an exceptional strength of character that is a negation of a good leadership. It does not bother him in the least that his practically wrong actions and leadership have reduced Cameroonians into a poverty-stricken people, eroded their sense of purpose, divided their ranks, rendered them into the grips of despondence, denigrated their influence in national and international politics, and encouraged corruption to the form of an art; and above all, it suits his propose that he has wrapped Cameroon into the clutch and whims of France.

After becoming the president in 1982, Biya has ruled Cameroon more like an absentee caretaker than even an absentee landlord. A two-month trip abroad for amusement using the taxpayer's money is unprecedented from any head of state. Nevertheless, it surprises only those who have no insight into his personality. Biya committed moral suicide years ago and now lacks the morality that is expected from a head of state. His rule has shattered the bilateral respect that prevailed between the different generations.

From peasant origins, Biya has learned, but wrongly assimilated aristocratic values. The sad result of this is his blatant and unjustifiable contempt of the masses from where he had his origins. As a man of high learning, it is unfortunate that despite his long years of service in the system, he still possesses all the traits of a pseudo-intellectual and a pedant. And it is due to his awareness of his intellectual feebleness that he has developed a masked inferiority complex. That is why he rejects, snubs and shies away from the good ideas of his intellectual superiors.

Cameroon is the only nation in Africa where its true liberation fighters and nationalists were never permitted to the helm of power. It is the first nation in Africa where France became deeply involved in collaboration with Ahidjo, in the genocide of those who resisted its deception (close to a million deaths in the 1956-1970 war against the UPC). Cameroon is the only country in Africa, which has been the most cruelly raped in our modern times by France. Even though Cameroonians are one of the most dynamic people in the continent, they have never been left to their devices to harness their potentials and build their country into the great nation that it truly deserves. Instead, Cameroonians have been brought low by a conspiracy hatched during the years of Jacques Foccart's control of

French policy on Africa, a conspiracy that has effectively used Cameroonian collaborators, especially Paul Biya.

It does not bother the second Cameroonian president in the least that the Cameroonian people are suffocating in his bondage. He has lost touch with the Cameroonian masses, the Cameroonian reality, and life in its different forms. However, unlike his psychopathic counterpart, the Roman emperor Nero, he has mastered one art—the art of retaining power despite the opposition from the masses. And as most megalomaniacs and experimentalists, he would continue to experiment with his theory of power retention, despite his unpopularity, not worried that the Cameroonian people are being dragged into the abyss in the process.

Biya is performing his theory of power retention on us, an experiment that will go a long way to destroy the best of our creative forces if left to persist. Moreover, with that will be the destruction of the faith we have in our dream and worst still the mother of progress, which is hope. The sad result of the disaster of Biya's rule would be the death of Cameroon. To the rational mind, that is unacceptable.

Perhaps for a little while longer, the living specter of the second Cameroonian president will continue to haunt the people—treacherous in his ways, ruthless in his methods and nonchalant in his views. It is our unavoidable task, if only for the sake of our children, that we rise up— take back our dignity, hope and future from him and his patrons. Then following the natural course of history, we shall confine him and his legacy to the dustbin of history.

February 28, 1995   *Janvier Tchouteu*

CHAPTER TWO

Longest Serving Heads of State in Africa and the Rest of the World

Rank	Name	Country	Office	Tenure Began	Length of Tenure
1	Paul Biya	Cameroon	Prime Minister, then President	30 June 1975	43 Years
2	Teodoro Obiang Nguema Mbasogo	Equatorial Guinea	President[1]	3 August 1979	38 Years

3	Ali Khamenei	Iran	President, then Supreme Head	13 October 1981	36 Years
4	Denis Sassou Nguesso	Republic of Congo	President	25 October 1997	18 Years
5	Hun Sen	Cambodia	Prime Minister[2]	14 January 1985	33 Years
6	Yoweri Museveni	Uganda	President	29 January 1986	32 Years
7	Nursultan Nazarbayev	Kazakhstan	Première Secrétaire et, then President	22 June 1989	29 Years
8	Omar al-Bashir	Sudan	President[3]	30 June 1989	29 Years
9	Idriss Déby	Chad	President[4]	2 December	27 Years

			]	1990	
10	Isaias Afwerki	Eritrea	President[5]	27 April 1991	27 Years
11	Emomali Rahmon	Tajikistan	President	19 November 1992	25 Years
12	Paul Kagame	Rwanda	President	19 July 1994	24 Years
13	Alexander Lukashenko	Belarus	President	20 July 1994	24 Years
14	Milo Đukanović	Montenegro	Prime Minister, then President	02/15/1991-11/25/2002 and 01/08/2003-11/10/2006 and 02/29/2008-12/29/2010 and	22 Years

18			President	05/20/2018 – present	
15	Mahathir Mohamad	Malaysia	Prime Minister	07/16/1981-10/31/2003 and 05/10/2018 – present	22 Years
16	Daniel Ortega	Nicaragua	President	03/04/1981-04/25/ 1990 and 01/10/2007 – present	20 Years
17	Tuilaepa Aiono Sailele Malielegaoi	Samoa	Prime Minister	23 November 1998	19 Years
17	Abdelaziz Bouteflika	Algeria	President	27 April 1999	19 Years
18	Ismaïl Omar Guelleh	Djibouti	President	8 May 1999	19 Years

19	Vladimir Putin	Russia	President[101]	9 August 1999	19 Years
20	Keith Mitchell	Grenada	Prime Minister	06/22/1995- 07/09 2008 and 02/20/2013- present	18 Years
21	Hage Geingob	Namibia	Prime Minister, then President	03/21/1990- 08/ 28/2002 and 12/04/2012- – present	18 Years
22	Bashar al-Assad	Syria	President	17 July 2000	18 Years
23	Joseph Kabila	The Democratic Republic of the Congo	President	17 January 2001	17 Years

24	Ralph Gonsalves	Saint Vincent and the Grenadines	Prime Minister	29 March 2001	17 Years
25	Barnabas Sibusiso Dlamini	Swaziland	Prime Minister	07/26/1996- 09/29/ 2003 and 10/23/2008 – présent	17 Years
26	Dési Bouterse	Surinam	President	02/25/1980- 01/25/ 1988 and 08/12/ 2010 – present	15 Years
27	Recep Tayyip Erdoğan	Turkey	Prime Minister, then President	14 March 2003	15 Years
28	Ilham Aliyev	Azerbaijan	Prime Minister, then	4 August 2003	15 Years

			President[1][2]		
29	Shavkat Mirziyoyev	Uzbekistan	Prime Minister, then President	11 December 2003	14 Years
30	Sheikh Hasina	Bangladesh	Prime Minister	06/231996- 07/ 15/ 2001 and 01/6 2009 – présent	14 Years
31	Roosevelt Skerrit	Dominica	Prime Minister	8 January 2004	14 Years
32	Mahmoud Abbas	Palestine	Prime Minister, then President	03/19/2003- 09/06/2003 01/15/2005 – present	12 Years
33	Lee Hsien Loong	Singapore	Prime Minister	12 August 2004	13 Years

34	Tommy Remengesau	Palau	President	01/01/2001- 01/15/2009 and 01/17/ 2013 – présent	13 Years
35	Faure Gnassingbé	Togo	President[15]	4 May 2005	13 Years
36	Salva Kiir Maiardit	South Sudan	President[16]	30 July 2005	13 Years
37	Pierre Nkurunziza	Burundi	President	26 August 2005	13 Years
38	Angelina Merkel	Germany	Chancelier Fédéral	22 November 2005	12 Years
39	Evo Morales	Bolivia	President	22 January 2006	12 Years

40	Benjamin Netanyahu	Israel	Prime Minister	06/18/1996- 07/0 6/1999 and 03/31/ 2009 – present	12 Years
41	Viktor Orban	Hungary	Prime Minister	07/06/1998 – 05/27/2002 and 05/29/2010 – present	12 Years
41	Doris Leuthard	Switzerland	Member of the Federation Council, erstwhile President	1 August 2006	11 Years
42	Frank Bainimarama	Fiji	Interim Pesident, then Prime Minister	05/29/2000- 07/13/ 2000 and 12/5/2006 –	11 Years

				present	
43	Gurbanguly Berdimuhamedow	Turkmenistan	President	21 December 2006	11 Years
44	Ibrahim Boubacar Keïta	Mali	Prime Minister, then President	02/04/1994-02/15/2000 and 09/04/2013 – present	10 Years
45	Bako Sahakyan	Artsakh (ancienne République du Haut-Karabakh)	President	7 September 2007	10 Years
46	Alassane Ouattara	Côte d'Ivoire	Prime Minister, then President	11/07/1990-11/ 9/ 1993 and 12/04/2010-present (2nd time)	10 Years

47	Dean Barrow	Belize	Prime Minister	8 February 2008	10 Years
48	Dmitry Medvedev	Russie	President, then Prime Minister	07 May 2008	10 Years

CHAPTER THREE

Salaries of heads of state and government of Countries in Africa and the Rest of the World

State	Head of state (USD)	Head of government (USD)
Cameroon	620,976 (President)[4] (Paul Biya)	
Afghanistan	13,400 (President)[1]	
Albania	19,665 (President)[2]	
Algeria	168,000 (President)[3][4]	
Andorra		82,800 (Prime Minister)[5]
Angola	60,000 (President)[3]	

State	Head of state (USD)	Head of government (USD)
Antigua and Barbuda	40,225 (Governor-General)[6]	
Argentina	130,000 (President)[7][8]	
Armenia	32,400 (President)[9]	
Australia	425,000 (Governor-General)	507,340 (Prime Minister)[10]
Austria	410,000 (President)[11]	328,600 (Chancellor)[11]
Azerbaijan	225,000 (President)[12]	
Bahamas		86,000 (Prime Minister)[13]
Bahrain		
Bangladesh	17,100 (President)[14]	16,400 (Prime Minister)[15]

State	Head of state (USD)	Head of government (USD)
Barbados		101,588 (Prime Minister)[16]
Cameroon	620,976 (President)[4] (Paul Biya)	
Belarus	33,600 (President)[17]	
Belgium	14,454,440 (King) royal grant[11]	262,964 (Prime Minister)[11]
Belize	26,241 (Governor-General)[18]	
Benin	29,810 (President)[4]	
Bhutan		37,365 (Prime Minister)[19]
Bolivia	39,924 (President)[8]	
Bosnia and	42,650 (Presidency)[20]	

State	Head of state (USD)	Head of government (USD)
Herzegovina		
Botswana	65,760 (President)[4]	
Brazil	120,000 (President)[21]	
Brunei		
Bulgaria	79,000 (President)[22]	50,000 (Prime Minister)[23]
Burkina Faso	33,810 (President)[4]	
Burundi	47,300 (President)[4]	
Cambodia		30,000 (Prime Minister)[24]
Cameroon	620,976 (President)[4]	
Canada	290,000 (Governor-	260,200 (Prime

State	Head of state (USD)	Head of government (USD)
	General)[25]	Minister)[4]
Cape Verde	20,380 (President)[4]	
Central African Republic	42,524 (President)[26]	
Chad		
Chile	180,000 (President)[11]	
China	22,000 (President)[27]	
Colombia	134,676 (President)[8]	
Comoros	117,060 (President)[4]	
Congo, Democratic Republic of the	51,500 (President)[4]	
Republic of Congo	108,400 (President)[4]	

State	Head of state (USD)	Head of government (USD)
Costa Rica	113,520 (President)[8]	
Croatia	45,200 (President)[28]	
Cuba	360 (President)[29]	
Cyprus	90,025 (President)[30]	
Czech Republic	11,477 (President)[31][11]	9,243 (Prime Minister)[32]
Denmark	11,350,744 (Queen) royal grant[33][5]	249,774 (Prime Minister)[11]
Djibouti		
Dominica		
Dominican Republic	120,000 (President)[34][8]	

State	Head of state (USD)	Head of government (USD)
East Timor	30,000 (President)[35]	27,000 (Prime Minister)[36]
Ecuador	75,132 (President)[37][8]	
Egypt	70,400 (President)[3]	
El Salvador	62,172 (President)[8]	
Equatorial Guinea	152,680 (President)[4]	
Eritrea		
Estonia	74,595 (President)[38][11]	74,595 (Prime Minister)[39]
Ethiopia	45,270 (President)[4]	44,470 (Prime Minister)[40]
Fiji	62,784 (President)[41]	113,495 (Prime Minister)[42]

State	Head of state (USD)	Head of government (USD)
Finland	155,285 (President)[11]	154,000 (Prime Minister)[43]
France	194,300 (President)[21]	220,500 (Prime Minister)[11]
Gabon	65,000 (President)[3]	
Gambia, The	65,000 (President)[3]	
Georgia	80,400 (President)[44]	
Germany	240,933 (President)[45]	299,784 (Chancellor)[45]
Ghana	76,000 (President)[3]	
Greece	154,739 (President)[17]	82,405 (Prime Minister)[11]
Grenada		24,797 (Prime Minister)[46]

State	Head of state (USD)	Head of government (USD)
Guatemala	178,680 (President)[8]	
Guinea	22,390 (President)[4]	
Guinea-Bissau		
Guyana	91,700 (President)[47]	98,300 (Prime Minister)[48]
Haiti	3,782 (President)[49]	
Honduras	49,908 (President)[8]	
Hong Kong	639,650 (Chief Executive)	
Hungary	70,964 (President)[11]	99,349 (Prime Minister)[11]
Iceland	191,000 (President)	242,619 (Prime Minister)[11]

State	Head of state (USD)	Head of government (USD)
India	₹60 lakh (US$87,000) (President)[50]	₹19 lakh (US$28,000) (Prime Minister)[21]
Indonesia	124,171 (President)[51]	
Iran		18,947 (President)[52]
Iraq	809,673 (President)[12]	
Ireland	401,000 (President)[53]	237,000 (Taoiseach)[54]
Israel	173,000 (President)[11]	168,210 (Prime Minister)[11]
Italy	275,147 (President)[21]	131,608 (Prime Minister)[17]
Ivory Coast	100,000 (President)[3]	
Jamaica		48,000 (Prime Minister)[55]

State	Head of state (USD)	Head of government (USD)
Japan	3,086,890 (Emperor) royal grant[11]	202,700 (Prime Minister)[21][11]
Jordan		
Kazakhstan	20,400 (President)[56][57]	2,630 (Ministers)[58]
Kenya	132,000 (President)[10][3][4]	
Kiribati	9,328 (President)[59]	
Kuwait		
Kyrgyzstan	18,800 (President)[60]	12,800 (Prime Minister)[61]
Laos		
Latvia	70,718 (President)[11]	59,644 (Prime Minister)[11]

State	Head of state (USD)	Head of government (USD)
Lebanon	150,000 (President)[62]	150,000 (Prime Minister)[63]
Lesotho		36,650 (Prime Minister)[4]
Liberia	90,000 (President)[3]	
Libya	105,000 (President)[3]	
Liechtenstein	0 (Prince)[5]	254,660 (Prime Minister)[64]
Lithuania	86,136 (President)[3]	50,100 (Prime Minister)
Luxembourg	12,333,102 (Grand Duke) royal grant[5]	278,000 (Prime Minister)[11]
Macedonia	17,250 (President)[65]	
Madagascar		

State	Head of state (USD)	Head of government (USD)
Malawi	74,300 (President)[4]	
Malaysia	263,500 (Yang di-Pertuan Agong)[66]	61,844 (Prime Minister)[67][68]
Maldives	78,074.17 (President)	
Mali	68,900 (President)[4]	
Malta	70,955 (President)[69]	56,900 (Prime Minister)[70]
Marshall Islands	90,000 (President)[71]	
Mauritania		
Mauritius	93,783 (President)[72]	187,968 (Prime Minister)[73]
Mexico	166,797 (President)[11]	

State	Head of state (USD)	Head of government (USD)
Micronesia	32,000 (President)[74]	30,000 (Vice President)[75]
Moldova	9,264 (President) [76]	6,433 (Prime Minister) [77]
Monaco	52,063,000 (Prince) royal grant[5]	
Mongolia	9,132 (President) [78]	8,940 (Prime Minister) [79]
Montenegro	33,440 (President)[80]	
Morocco	488,604 (King)[4]	
Mozambique	46,800 (President)[4]	
Myanmar	60,000 (President)[81]	
Namibia	99,241 (President)[82][4]	76,339 (Prime Minister)[82]

State	Head of state (USD)	Head of government (USD)
Nauru	74,411 (President)[83]	
Nepal	17,584 (President)[84]	9,033 (Prime Minister)[84]
Netherlands	6,082,736 (King) royal grant[85][5]	193,844 (Prime Minister)[11]
New Zealand	260,245 (Governor-General)[11]	325,546 (Prime Minister)[10]
Nicaragua	38,316 (President)[8]	
Niger		
Nigeria	69,000 (President)[4]	
North Korea		
Norway	33,237,000 (King) royal grant[5]	210,714 (Prime Minister)[11]

State	Head of state (USD)	Head of government (USD)
Oman		
Pakistan	46,600 (President)[86]	
Palau	50,000 (President)[87][88]	
Palestine		
Panama	84,000 (President)[8]	
Papua New Guinea		107,532 (Prime Minister)[89]
Paraguay	103,044 (President)[8]	
Peru	57,168 (President)[8]	
Philippines	95,554 (President)[90]	
Poland	70,026 (President)[11]	57,772 (Prime

State	Head of state (USD)	Head of government (USD)
		Minister)[11]
Portugal	96,469 (President)[11]	72,352 (Prime Minister)[11]
Qatar		
Romania	61,296 (President)[91]	61,296 (Prime Minister)[91]
Russia	136,000 (President)[21]	105,000 (Prime Minister)[92]
Rwanda	85,000 (President)[3]	
Saint Kitts and Nevis		
Saint Lucia		
Saint Vincent and the Grenadines		

State	Head of state (USD)	Head of government (USD)
Samoa	82,000 (Head of State)[93]	78,000 (Prime Minister)[94]
San Marino	83,682 (Both Captain Regents)[95]	
São Tomé and Príncipe		
Saudi Arabia		
Senegal	15,210 (President)[4]	
Serbia	14,950 (President)[96]	
Seychelles	24,600 (President)[97]	
Sierra Leone	12,220 (President)[4]	
Singapore	1,142,000 (President)[98]	1,631,000 (Prime Minister)[10]

State	Head of state (USD)	Head of government (USD)
Slovakia	129,284 (President)[99]	70,973 (Prime Minister)[11]
Slovenia	80,142 (President)[11]	87,818 (Prime Minister)[11]
Solomon Islands		18,181 (Prime Minister)[100]
Somalia	120,000 (President)[101]	
South Africa	223,500 (President)[21][4]	
South Korea	210,000 (President)[11]	
South Sudan	60,000 (President)[102]	
Spain	3,311,000 (King) royal grant[103][5]	97,926 (Prime Minister)[11]
Sri Lanka	7,380 (President)[104]	5,600 (Prime Minister)[105]

State	Head of state (USD)	Head of government (USD)
Sudan	29,320 (President)[4]	
Suriname	133,560 (President)[106][107]	116,870 (Vice President)[108]
Swaziland		51,600 (Prime Minister)[4][109]
Sweden	15,752,000 (King) royal grant[5]	244,615 (Prime Minister)[11]
Switzerland	507,000 (President)[110]	495,000 (Federal Council)[111]
Syria		
Tajikistan	13,200 (President)[112][113]	
Tanzania	47,300 (President)[4]	
Thailand		49,728 (Prime Minister)[114]

State	Head of state (USD)	Head of government (USD)
Togo		
Tonga	2,129,540 (King) royal grant[115]	41,504 (Prime Minister)[116]
Trinidad and Tobago		85,600 (Prime Minister)[117]
Tunisia	16,700 (President)[4]	
Turkey	197,400 (President)[21]	
Turkmenistan		
Tuvalu	17,660 (Governor-General)[118]	19,808 (Prime Minister)[119]
Uganda	183,216 (President)[4]	
Ukraine	11,600 (President)[120]	3,840 (Prime Minister)[121]

State	Head of state (USD)	Head of government (USD)
United Arab Emirates		
United Kingdom	107,392,287 (Queen) royal grant[11]	215,980 (Prime Minister)[21][11]
United States	400,000 (President)[4]	
Uruguay	139,608 (President)[8]	
Uzbekistan	15,600 (President)[122][123]	
Vanuatu	32,295 (President)[124]	32,295 (Prime Minister)[125]
Vatican City	0 (Pope)[5]	
Venezuela	48,816 (President)[8]	
Vietnam		9,660 (Prime Minister)[126]

State	Head of state (USD)	Head of government (USD)
Yemen		
Zambia	64,000 (President)[4]	
Zimbabwe	146,590 (President)[4]	

CHAPTER FOUR

Africa's Haunted Heart

A specter looms in the lives of every Cameroonian child, man or woman. It is the living president of the land in the middle of Africa, the land that is often referred to as the microcosm of the continent. The specter is President Paul Biya of Cameroon. When rumors spread like wildfire in June 2004 that he had just died, there were widespread scenes of jubilation all across the half a million square kilometer landmass called Cameroon. Days after the circulation of the unverified account, he returned home from abroad where he had been passing his time, intermittently, about six months every year for over two decades, and then declared to the sycophants waiting to receive him at the airport that there would be a .... "Rendez-vous in 20 years' time with those who wish me dead..."

Cameroonians were not the only ones who disbelieved him when he made that pronouncement among other things. Many of those who follow political developments in the world in general, and in Africa and Cameroon in particular, marveled at his audacity. After all, more than 80% of the Cameroonian population loathed his rule; he was already in power for more than two decades as the head of state, after having been the country's prime minister (1972-1982) or the second most powerful person in the system put in place in Cameroon by the French overlords.

But Paul Biya proved everyone wrong. He pulled off another electoral charade and declared himself the winner in the October 2004 presidential election, and then changed his constitution in 2008 that would allow him to run for two more presidential 7-year terms (despite the deaths of 150 protesting Cameroonians caused by his armed forces), meaning that he could be president until the year 2025 (a record of 43 years in power) when he would be 92 years of age.

That explains why by the time Paul Biya held another masquerade called presidential elections in October 2011, he had already successfully humbled the internationally recognized opposition heads (who are all former members of the country's sole political party from 1972-1990, a party Biya has been leading since 1984), promised to give them positions in his government and made it known in plain terms that the system string-controlled by the puppeteer (France) would never allow political change in Cameroon that would curtail France's unrestricted interests in the African country.

The octogenarian Paul Biya is variously described as the Maradona (he fakes and wins elections just like Maradona faked and scored a goal in his "Hand of God" goal) of Cameroonian and African politics, the master of presidential patricide (he devoured his predecessor who passed over power to him, leading to the first Cameroonian president Ahmadou Ahidjo's exile, death and burial abroad—Senegal), the absentee president, the vindictive president, the evil president, etc. etc.

As a German colony from 1884-1916, Kamerun was often referred to by the German Colonial administration and the imperial-minded in the Kaiser's Germany as an "African Pearl", owing to the colony's robust economy, highest literacy rate in the continent in the early 1900s, magnificent physical features, rich and varied vegetation cover, and also owing to its diverse ethnic ethnicities that included all the major language groups in Africa (Afro-Asia, Niger-Congo-A, Niger-Congo-B or Bantu, and Nilo-Saharan. in fact, historians consider the German colony of Kamerun as a major part of Adolf Hitler's rue over the territories Germany lost after the First World because of the peace terms imposed on it by the victories Allied Powers during the Versailles Conference. As it happens, one of the peace terms imposed on the post-Kaiser Germany was the loss of German Kamerun to Britain and France. That was how Kamerun was partitioned into British Cameroons and French Cameroon.

As a matter of fact, the French Cameroun mandate became France's most valuable assets in Sub-Saharan Africa. Its value was validated even further when the territory became the Launchpad of French General Charles De Gaulle-led Free French Forces that wrestled French Equatorial Africa from the Nazi puppet regime of Vichy France during the Second World War. This force would gallantly fight alongside Allied Forces against Italian and

German forces in Libya, Tunisia and the Middle East, before carrying on to Italy and France where their biggest achievement was the liberation of Paris. The fact that French Camerounians played an invaluable role in the war effort to liberate France from Nazi Germany makes the explanation simple as to why French Camerounian soldiers returned home and sought self-government, liberty, democracy, reunification with British Cameroons that would culminate in the independence of the two United Nations Trust Territories. They were merely seeking the rights that they had helped France to regain from Nazi Germany, which is why pundits were not surprised at all.

The formation of the UPC (Union of the Populations of the Camerouns) in French Cameroun in 1946 and the birth of sister union-nationalist (civic-nationalist) parties in British Cameroons highlighted the seriousness of the former Kamerunians to work together to build a "New Cameroon". By 1955, the UPC commanded more than 80% of popular support in French Cameroun.

So pundits considered it foolhardy when the French government issued a decree banning the UPC on July 13, 1955, in French Cameroons, a strategic act that was followed by the party's ban in British Cameroons three years later on the same fabricated charges of inciting violence and for being communists. These coordinated moves by Africa's two foremost colonial masters at the time were supposed to spell disaster for the dream held by Cameroon's leaders. Many Cameroonians saw nothing but duplicity and hypocrisy in the moves, wondering whether the freedom they had assisted the Free French Forces to achieve for France and its citizens was a special right or privilege meant for "White People" only.

When in 1956, the UPC resorted to a partisan war of liberation from French rule, it was a belated move to confront France after failing to resolve the ban in a peaceful manner. That war would end with the defeat of the UPC in 1970, a defeat that came with the assassinations and execution of the party's successive heads in 1958, 1960 and 1971, i.e., the deaths of Ruben Um Nyobe, Dr. Felix Moumie, and Ernest Ouandie respectively. It would leave Cameroon entrapped through a French-imposed system rooted in the Colonial Pact France made its puppets sign before allowing their countries to become members of the United Nations Organization by granting these former colonies string-controlled independence.

Despite the period of instability during the country's unsuccessful war of liberation that saw the French Trusteeship masters handing power to those who never asked for or never fought for it (the puppets that constitute the system today), despite the eventual peaceful reunification of British Southern Cameroons with the former French Cameroun, despite Cameroon's agricultural recovery and the discovery of oil in the 1970s that saw the country emerge as Africa's eight largest economy and the world's second fastest growing in the early 1980s, Cameroon is today in a horrible shape.

The Cameroonian economy that was expected to grow twenty times over the next thirty years, i.e., from 1982-2012, barely doubled over that period of time. Everything changed for the worse after Paul Biya was handed power in

November 1982 by the first French-installed puppet Cameroonian president Ahmadou Ahidjo. Since then, Cameroon has experienced the biggest proportionate embezzlement of state funds ever recorded in Africa. And the country holds the sad record as the country in Africa that has experienced the worst peacetime impoverishment since 1960.

Today, president Paul Biya is presiding over a nation where more than 80% of its physicians are abroad, where more than 90% of its doctorate degree holders are abroad, where Cameroonians invest abroad more than at home, where Cameroonians are voting against the system with their feet; today, Cameroon's neighbors who before envied its high standards of living and saw it as a place of refuge and opportunities, now find Cameroonians envying them as they forge ahead with a sense of direction while Cameroon lags behind in its spiral towards total, complete and horrifying economic, social and political decay.

People unfamiliar with the Cameroonian situation would be wondering why such an abysmal situation persists. Well; the answer is simple. Cameroon finds itself today in a situation like someone in a quicksand because of the anachronistic system put in place by Gaullist France when General Charles De Gaulle returned to power in 1958 and decided to make France's former colonies and territories members of the United Nations Organization (UNO), while controlling them with transparent or invisible strings this time. French Cameroun and British Southern Cameroons achieved independence and reunification all right, only for the people to find that the new country is quasi-independent under a broader French template of control variously described as FrancAfrique. This French-imposed system has traumatized, demoralized, divided and dehumanized the Cameroonian people over the years.

The Gaullist system put in place by the elites of the French political establishment has as one of its major objectives the exclusion from Cameroon's political power of the union-nationalists advocating for the reunification and independence of the divided territories of the former German Kamerun, civic nationalists who commanded the support of more than 80% of the populations of both territories of British Cameroons and French Cameroun in the 1950s and 1960s. The current system in Cameroon is a partnership of French imperial interest in Africa (economic and political) otherwise known as FrancAfrique and its Cameroonian collaborators (the renegades and anti-union-nationalists who never opposed and who do not object to France's neo-colonial stranglehold of Cameroon).

The system has been effective in infecting the minds of many Cameroonians, reducing them into a state of hopelessness, in a process that lures them to direct their energy not against the Biya regime and the system, but at their neighbors. The system has successfully elevated corruption and the divide-and-rule strategy into an art—it has promoted the notion of settlers and indigenes, it has encouraged ethnocentrism, tribalism, clannishness, regional jingoism, sectarianism and other forms of division. We see a total and complete absence of strategic or even tactical planning when it comes to the economic and social development of the nation. We see a complete absence of social solidarity.

To compound the division and confusion among the people who reject the Biya regime and the French-imposed system, the so-called opposition leaders these freedom-craving Cameroonians had been looking up to have now been absorbed back into the system, leaving the struggling Cameroonian masses distrustful of politicians in general. Today, the down-trodden Cameroonian people are in a state of political lethargy.

When Paul Biya called for the holding of Senate elections in April 2013, eighteen years after his parliament promulgated a law to create one, most Cameroonians thought it would be another charade, as usual. It made no sense for the so-called opposition parties with a semblance of representation in parliament to glorify the charade with their participation. Most Cameroonians knew the system was sustaining these so-called opposition leaders financially and that some of them were in the government, but Cameroonians were not prepared for the extent to which these politicians would go to insult their intelligence. But deals between the ruling party and the opposition were made all right. The electoral masquerade took place and the people saw the ruling party campaigning for the so-called main opposition party (Social Democratic Front—SDF) in some regions of the country, while the SDF in the words of its chairman or president John Fru Ndi "…one good turn deserves another…", openly backed the ruling party, thereby ensuring its victory in other regions of the country.

How could that have happened? Politically-shocked Cameroonians have been asking themselves ever since the open fornication between the ruling party and the so-called opposition political parties in April 2013.

To prevent chaos and ensure a smooth succession, SDF spokes-persons, and apologists quip.

"Paul Biya has a deal with the SDF to hand over power to one of its members," some anonymous voices within the SDF echo.

If you ask me, my answer is clear. What was supposed to be a Cameroonian revolution that began on May 26, 1990, became a political comedy played by former members of the French-imposed system or political establishment, a political comedy that has gone full circle. The worldwide wind of change generated by Mikhail Gorbachev's Glasnost and Perestroika that swept away authoritarian systems in Eastern Europe and Africa, and that stirred the vast majority of Cameroonians in the 1990s to risk their lives in the streets demanding political change, was effectively controlled by the system. The desire for change that more than 80% of Cameroonians have has been hijacked by the authoritarian system in Cameroon and the so-called leaders of the opposition. The people got taken for a ride.

The biggest mistake made by Cameroonians was that when the clamor for change began, they followed Cameroonians who had no democratic credentials, people who hardly a year before, were in the upper echelons of power in the system, but who at the time claimed they had left the ruling party and now opposed it. All the so-called heads of what the world knows today as the prominent opposition parties in Cameroon (John Fru Ndi of the SDF,

Bello Bouba Maigari of the UNDP, Ndam Njoya of the CDU etc.) were members of the ruling party right up to the year 1990, when the system was forced to accept multi-party politics in Cameroon. Like the Pied Piper, these so-called opposition leaders lured freedom-starved Cameroonians into greater despondence and political lethargy. Such a feat was achieved only because Cameroonian liberals, union-nationalists, revolutionaries, democrats and patriots who had always rejected the system, thought these so-called heads of the so-called new opposition, these people who were the first to make the moves to create political parties, shared the vision of the "New Cameroon" that Cameroonians fought, died and voted for, a vision that achieved the land's reunification and independence (though it has never been real because it got usurped by the evil system that today is under the leadership of Paul Biya and his French puppeteers.), but that is yet to realize democracy, freedom, liberalism, progress, justice, equality and development.

False are the statements by members of the compromised opposition that had they not openly embraced the Biya regime and the system, chaos would have ensued in Cameroon incase Biya exited the political scene. There is no truth in the statement because the system in Cameroon is authoritarian, not autocratic.

Authoritarian regimes are usually coated with a sublime idea that could be political (Stalinism/Marxism/Communism, Fascism etc.), that could be religious (Iranian and Taliban theocracy etc.) or that could be an interest arrangement (FrancAfrique). in

Cameroon, the system is built around preventing those who believe in the Cameroonian struggle (the union-nationalists, otherwise called the Kamerunists) from attaining power.

The system in Cameroon is a collection of individual interest groups, bringing together the propagators of French neo-colonialism and their Cameroonian collaborators. Paul Biya is the head of the collaborationists. And in many ways, he has been acting over the years as an absentee president. Meanwhile, the state has been functioning zombie-like during his quasi-presence. As a matter of fact, even though the mortifying arrangement suited the interest of the puppeteers and the beneficiaries of the system, it exposed the system to popular uprisings since that means the beneficiaries of the system are not clearly or functionally organized. With the advent of social media, globalization, the maturity of post-independence generations that never benefited from the system; and with the soldiers of the 1990s phase of the struggle dissociating themselves from the so-called opposition leaders, the authoritarian system now finds itself even more vulnerable.

The authoritarian system would be faced by a new political force that never associated itself with the system, a new political force that embodies the spirit of the century-old struggle for the "NEW KAMERUN" or "NEW CAMEROON" that confronted German colonial control, stood up to French duplicity in the land in a war that decimated more than half a million of its supporters; the authoritarian system would be faced by a new force that embraces the legacy of those who fought, died and voted for the independence and reunification of Cameroon, a new force that rejects all the values of the system that the French political mafia over Africa put in place in their game plan to control the destiny of Cameroon, a six-decade-old evil system that can only lead the country to abyss.

Now, as the open and hidden collaborators of the system openly embrace one another (the ruling party and the so-called heads of the so-called opposition parties) starting with the recent senatorial charade where the so-called principal opposition—the Social Democratic Front (SDF) and the party of Paul Biya—Cameroon People's Democratic Movement (CPDM) supported each other's aspirations in agreed-upon provinces with guaranteed votes from party members, the system is encouraging the creation of elite groups of beneficiaries who see or think that their political and economic survival rests only in a continuation or sustenance of the system. We are observing the evolvement of a system that is shedding any pretense of limited political pluralism; we are observing the entrenchment of a system that openly views the people as its number one enemy. Such a system then becomes autocratic.

In a nutshell, Cameroon's so-called opposition political parties that are in symbiosis with the authoritarian system are aiding the system in its gradual transition into an autocratic system, thereby ensuring its survival in a morphed form. The rapidly changing system needs a strong man to be truly autocratic. This would be someone who has hands on the job to act as the president, someone who the French puppeteers would like to portray as the benevolent despot.

As Egyptian writer Alaa Al -Aswany said, "The concept of the benevolent dictator, just like the concepts of the noble thief or the honest whore, is no more than a meaningless fantasy."

It is the place of post-independence Cameroonians to reject whatever farce the system comes up with as change whenever power passes down to the generation after Paul Biya. By absorbing former members of his party who for decades identified with the opposition, Biya is trying to give Cameroonians and the rest of the world the impression that Cameroon's opposition is in sync with his vision for the political evolution of Cameroon. Unfortunately, the system does not intend to let the majority of Cameroonians participate or have a say in Cameroon's political development or evolution.

The New Cameroon will be founded. Not by beneficiaries of the system (past and present) but by those who have always rejected it as an evil system that has been leading Cameroon into the abyss.

But then, in founding the New Cameroon, patriotic, honest, democratic, unbiased and progressive-minded Cameroonians would have to reconcile a country where:

- the system made sure that most of its historic figures who dedicated their lives and even died for the cause for Cameroon's reunification and independence got killed and buried like dogs at home and abroad,

- the bodies of some of these historic figures that got buried abroad are missing,
- a few of the historic figures who thought they could contribute in nation-building got sidelined, cowed and humiliated by the system,
- its first head of state died and is buried abroad,
- and where the people have been insulted for more than five decades by the regimes of Ahmadou Ahidjo and Paul Biya through an imposed minority system that sowed the seeds of division, corruption, mediocrity, fear, and despondency that are haunting Cameroon today.

The ideas and ideals of the New Cameroon hatched by the country's historic civic-nationalists and developed over the years by post-independence union-nationalists is Cameroon's only bargain with the future. It is the only nucleus around which Cameroon can reconcile with its turbulent past; it is the nucleus that all the strata of Cameroonian society can connect to in the process of nation-building; it is the only nucleus around which a free, democratic, liberal, fair and prosperous Cameroon can be built. The New Cameroon would lead the country in taking its merited place in the central African region, Africa as a whole, and the world at large. That would be possible only if we confine the legacies of the Ahidjo/Biya regimes and the suffocating French-imposed system to the dustbin of history.

Janvier Tchouteu   *06/04/2013*

CONCLUSION

Nowhere is the hope for the "NEW CAMEROON" glaringly manifested than in the country's National Football Team, which despite the constraints from the French-imposed system (poor infrastructure over the years, poor and corrupt management etc.), the National Football (National Soccer) Team has made Cameroon an exemplary and perhaps No 1 nation in Africa and one of the best in the world. The players never corrupted their compatriots, but gave in their best despite the odds stacked against them. They show the world that Cameroon has the potential to become Africa's light and not the black sheep that the political mafia France set up in the country called the political establishment has made the country to be perceived as for close to six decades.

Cameroon's Anglophone problem or better put, the plight of the two Anglophone provinces of the Northwest and the Southwest, the area that was formerly British Southern Cameroons, highlights the depravity of the system more than any other problem in the country. Yet, strangely enough, the forces that want to tear Cameroon apart and the forces that are running it down while appearing to oppose each other, help to make each other relevant. But the good thing is that these forces are a minority in every part of the country.

The forces that want to tear Cameroon apart are most visible in the English-speaking (Anglophone) part of the country. This force happens to be mostly those who voted against the reunification of British Southern Cameroons and *La Republique du Cameroun*---The Republic of Cameroun (The former French Cameroon) in 1961, and their descendants today. Their agenda to create an independent Southern Cameroons or Ambazonia is not accepted in Anglophone Cameroon (the former British Southern Cameroons, the former West Cameroon or the Northwest and Southwest regions today) by those who voted for reunification, most whom are Cameroonian civic-nationalists, otherwise called union-nationalists or Kamerunists. Most of the Anglophone Kamerunists would like to see a return to the 1961 two state federation of West Cameroon(English-speaking) and East Cameroon (French Speaking) or a federation of ten or more regions or states, just like most of the Francophone Kamerunists.

Unfortunately, the minority Southern Cameroon irredentists on the one hand and the minority usurper Cameroonian establishment set up by the French political mafia (Francaqfrique) on the other hand, are making each other relevant in their agendas as the anti-Cameroonian Biya regime cloaks the patriotic garment that it has stolen from Cameroon's historic union-nationalists and poses as the force that is trying to keep Cameroon together from the Southern Cameroon secessionists, while the Southern Cameroon irredentists undermine the Cameroonian union-nationalists on both sides of the River Wouri by posing as the force that is going to liberate Anglophone Cameroonians from "Francophones and their regime". Only by Cameroonian union-nationalists exposing and squashing the actions and agendas of both the usurper establishment and the Anglophone irredentists would the "New Cameroon" be born.

GLOSSARY ON CAMEROON

Adamawa	The southernmost province that was carved out of the former Grand North Province. It is a plateau region.
Akonolinga	A town in the Center Region. It is also the capital of the Nyong and Nfomou Division.
Akum	A Ngemba settlement 9 miles from Bamenda along the Bafoussam-Bamenda road. It is also a traditional Ngemba kingdom and the dialect of the people there.
Ambam	A town in the South Region. It is a sub-divisional capital in Ntem Division.
Ashia	Word used by both English and French-speaking Cameroonians to express sympathy, condolence, consolation, encouragement, compassion, harmony, understanding,

agreement, thankfulness, and caution.

Bafang   The capital of Upper Nkam Division
                      and a Bamileké kingdom in the West
                      Region.

Bafaw   The principal ethnic group in the area
                      that   comprises   the   Kumba
                      municipality. It is part of the larger
                      Bantu group.

Bafedja   A settlement and Bamileké kingdom
                      in the Nde or Banganté Division, West
                      Region.

Bafoussam   The capital of the West Region and
                      Mifi Division. Also a traditional
                      Bamileké kingdom.

Bafut   A settlement and traditional Ngemba
                      kingdom   about   18   miles   from
                      Bamenda in the Northwest Region.

Bakweri   The principal ethnic group in the Fako
                      Division, which is located in the
                      Southwest Region. The Bakwerians
                      are Bantu speaking of the Sawabantu
                      subgroup.

Balengou	Bamileké settlement and kingdom in the Nde Division, West Region.
Bali	A Chamba settlement and kingdom about 18 miles north of Bamenda, in the Northwest Region.
Bamena	Bamileké settlement and kingdom in the Nde Division, West Region.
Bambili	A settlement and Ngemba kingdom about 9 miles north of Bamenda in the Northwest Region.
Bambui	A Ngemba settlement and kingdom about 6 miles north of Bamenda in the Northwest Region.
Bamenda	The capital of the Northwest Region and Mezam Division.
Bamendjou	Bamileké settlement and kingdom in the Mifi Division, West Region.
Bami (Bamileké)	Diminutive of Bamileké.
Bamileké (Bami)	The most populous semi-Bantu ethnicity and the principal ethnic group in Cameroon. It is also their mother tongue.

Bamilekéland	The western half of the West Region, with fringes in the Northwest and Southwest Regions. It comprises five administrative divisions, about ninety traditional kingdoms, and eleven dialectical groupings.
Bamoun	A semi-Bantu ethnicity and one of the principal ethnic groups in Cameroon. Also their mother tongue.
Bamounland	The Eastern half of the Western province.
Bandekop	A Bamileké settlement and kingdom in Mifi Division, West Region.
Banganté	The largest Bamileké kingdom, the capital of Nde Division, its former name. Found in the West Region.
Bangou	A Bamileké settlement and kingdom in the Upper Nkam Division, West Region.
Bangoua	Bamileké settlement and kingdom in Nde Division, West Region.
Bangoulap	Bamileké settlement and kingdom in Nde Division, West Region.

Bantu

A Large group of Negroid peoples of Central, South, and East Africa that inhabits the forests of the Southwest, Littoral, Center, South, and East Regions of Cameroon. Also the largest constituent of the Negroid or Black race.

Bassa

The principal ethnic group in the Littoral Region. It is Bantu speaking. Also found in the Center Region of Cameroon.

Batoufam

Bamileké kingdom in the Mifi Division, West Region.

Bawok (Bahouok, Bahouoc)

Bamileké kingdoms speaking the Medumba dialects, found in the West and Northwest Regions. The principal ones are:

- Bawok-Banganté or Banganté-Bawok is a traditional Bamileké kingdom found in the Banganté subdivision, Nde Division. Much of the kingdom is located in the city of Banganté. Following a series of strives in the early twentieth century, it lost most of its territory to the surrounding Bamileké kingdoms, with its subjects migrating to other areas in Cameroon and even founding new kingdoms.

- Bawok-Bali or Bali-Bawok: An offshoot of the mother kingdom of Bawok-Banganté, founded in 1907 with the help of the friendly Bali-Nyonga kingdom. It is an enclave in the Bali kingdom (*fondom* or kingdom)

Bayangam   Bamileké settlement and kingdom in the Mifi Division, West Region.

Bazou   Bamileké kingdom in Nde Division, West Region.

Beti   Diminutive of Beti-Pahuin. It is also a subdivision of the Beti-Pahuin group of languages and is broken down further into Ewondo, Eton, Bane, Mbida-Mbane and Mvog-Nyenge.

Beti-Pahuin   Diminuted or shortened to Beti, this

group of related peoples constitutes the third principal ethnic group in Cameroon. The ethnic homeland of the Beti-Pahuin people is in the Center and South Regions, with fringes and enclaves in the East Region. They are Bantu-speaking and comprise the following:

- Beti (Ewondo, Bane, Mbida-Mbane, Mvog-Nyenge, and Eton),
- Fang (Fang proper, Ntumu, Mvae, and Okak)
- Bulu (Bulu, Fong, Mvele, Zaman, Yebekanga, Yengono, Yembama, Yelinda, Yesum, and Yekebolo.)
- Smaller tribes or ethnic groups Pahuinised by the Beti-Pahuins such as the Baka, Bamvele, Manguissa, Yekaba, Evuzok, Batchanga (Tsinga), Omvang, Yetude peoples.

Beti-Pahuin people are also indigenous in Equatorial Guinea, Gabon and The Republic of Congo.

Betiland

The Beti-Pahuin speaking regions of Cameroon (stretches from the southern half of the Center Region, to the central and eastern parts of the South Region and extend as fringes into the Eastern province), Equatorial Guinea (Rio Muni), Gabon (the northern half), The Republic of Congo (the Northwest), and São Tomé and Príncipe.

Biafra — The short-lived Ibo-dominated state that seceded from Nigeria during the 1966–1970 Nigerian Civil War.

Bota — A suburb of Limbe, Fako Division, Southwest Region.

British Cameroons — The western third of the former German Kamerun that fell under British control following the partition of the German colony. It comprised British Northern Cameroons and British Southern Cameroons.

Boumnyebel — A Bassa village in Nyong and Kelle Division, Center Region.

British Northern Cameroons — The Northern half of British Cameroons that voted to unite with Nigeria in 1961, following the controversial United Nations plebiscite in the territory.

British Southern Cameroons	The Southern half of British Cameroons. Became part of the Cameroon Federation in 1961 following a plebiscite that resulted in its reunification with the former French Cameroun. It comprises the Northwest and Southwest Regions of Cameroon.
Buea	The capital town of the Southwest Region and former capital of German Kamerun.
Bulu	One of the peoples of the Beti-Fang ethnic group with a homeland in the South Region.
Cameroonian Pidgin	Also called Cameroonian Creole or Kamtok, it is the Pidgin English spoken in Cameron. It has five variants.
CDU (Cameroon Democratic Union). Called *UDC (Union Démocratique du Cameroun)* in French	A political party in Cameroon founded by Adamou Ndam Njoya, a former minister of the Ahmadou Ahidjo regime.

CENER

(*Center National des Etudes et de Recherché*)—Acronym of Cameroon's secret intelligence service (National Center for Studies and Research)—that was changed in 1984 to *Direction Générale de la Recherché Extérieures (*DGRE)—General Directorate for External Research.

Center Region

Central province of Cameroon. Comprises eight divisions.

CNU (Cameroon National Union) called in French UNC *(Union Nationale Camerounaise)*

Party formed in 1966 from the merger of the political parties operating in Cameroon. It was headed by first Cameroonian president Ahmadou Ahidjo.

CPDM (Cameroon People's Democratic Movement), called in French RDPC *(Rassemblement Démocratique du Peuple Camerounais*)

The CNU renamed in 1985. This is the party in Cameroon. Its former name (1966-1985) was the Cameroon National Union (UNC), which itself was formed in 1966 by the merger of political parties in Cameroon. Before that, it was called the UC (*Union Camerounaise*)---Cameroonian Union (CU), the former political party founded by Ahmadou Ahidjo, the former President of the Republic of Cameroon. The CPDM/CNU/CU/UC

	has been the ruling party since the so-called 'independence of Cameroon in 1960. Paul Biya is the party's president.
CU (Cameroonian Union) called in French *UC (Union Camerounaise)*	Party formed by Ahmadou Ahidjo.
Douala	Largest city, economic capital and capital of Wouri division and Littoral Region.
Duala	A Bantu-speaking people of the Sawabantu subgroup, they are the principal ethnic group of the Wouri Division and the Douala area.
East Cameroon	The French-speaking federal unit of Cameroon from 1961–72. It was formed from the former French Cameroun.
East Region	The Southeastern half of Cameroon. The East Region has four divisions with Bertoua as its capital.
Eton	One of the peoples of the Beti-Fang ethnic group. Found in the Center

Region.

Ewondo

One of the peoples of the Beti-Fang group. Found in the Center Region of Cameroon.

Extreme North

A province in the far North of Cameroon. It comprises six divisions.

Free French Forces

These were French and Francophone fighters who continued fighting the axis powers of Germany, Italy, and Japan, even after France surrendered and signed an armistice agreement with Nazi Germany in June 1940. It was formed by General Charles De Gaulle, who was a member of the French cabinet on an official visit to Britain at the time of the surrender. General Charles De Gaulle strongly opposed French capitulation and the armistice signed by the new regime led by Marshall Petain that created the Vichy regime in the South of France, thereby allowing the North of the country to be under German occupation. He urged resistance against German control of France and its collaborationist Vichy puppets. The movement drew recruits mostly from the French empire, especially from French Central Africa, of which French Cameroun was the base at the time, under the new governorship of Jacques Philippe LeClerc. Philippe LeClerc led the Free French Forces' first major victory in the war with the capture in 1941 of Kufra, a town in the then Italian colony of Libya. It incorporated forces of the former Vichy regime in the colonies from 1943 and saw its ranks swollen by Frenchmen after the D-Day landing. The Free French Forces achieved their greatest glory with the liberation of Paris in August 1944, led by the French 2nd Armored Division because it had the least number of blacks in its ranks. By the end of the war, The Free French Movement constituted the fourth largest military force in Europe, fighting against the Axis powers. The right-wing political parties in France have been dominated by its members and the ideology of its founder called Gaullism.

FSD (Front Social-Démocrate). The SDF (Social Democratic — The political party that is described as the opposition leader in Cameroon. The SDF is led since its inception on

Front) in French.	May 26, 1990, by John Fru Ndi.
Fulfulde (Fula, Pulaar, Pular, Peul)	A Sene-Gambian language spoken by the Fulani people.
Fulani (Fulani, Fula, Fellata or Peul)	A mixed Negro-Tuareg people inhabiting the Savannah from Sudan to Sene-Gambia, they comprise three groups namely:

The Mbororo, Bororo, Burure or Abore who are pastoralists.

The Fulanin Gida, Ndoowi'en or Magida, who are fully sedentary communities.

The semi-sedentary Peul people who are agriculturalist and ultimately resume pastoralism, but often form permanent communities.

Foulanis, Fulanis or Peuls are the second most populous ethnic group in Cameroon. Found mostly in the northern provinces of Adamawa, North and Extreme North. Their language is the lingua franca of this part of Cameroon.

Foumbam	The capital of the Noun Division and

	the Bamounland. Found in the West Region.
Foumbot	Agricultural settlement in the Noun Division.
French Cameroun	The Eastern two third of the former German Kamerun that fell under the control of the French following the partition of the German colony by Britain and France. It became a French mandatory territory and later trust territory from 1918–1960.
Garoua	The capital of the North Region and Benue Division.
Graffi	Pidgin German word for a grass field. A name often applied collectively to the semi-Bantu peoples of the Northwest and West Regions of Cameroon.
Graffiland	Cameroonian word for Western High Plateau, Western Highlands, or Bamenda Grassfields. Mountainous grassland region of the Northwest and West Regions of Cameroon. It comprises the Bamilekéland and Bamounland in the south, and the

Ngembaland, Chambaland, and Tikarland in the north.

Ibo — One of the four principal ethnic groups of Nigeria. Found in the southeast.

Idenau — A town in Fako Division, Southwest Region.

Kamveu — The local council of notables among the different Bamileké kingdoms.

Koufra (Kufra) — An important but isolated Oasis settlement in the southeastern Libyan desert that was of strategic importance for the North African campaign during the Second World War. Its capture from the Italians by the Free French Forces marked the first major battle won by France in the war, thereby boosting General Charles De Gaulle's prestige and the morale of the demoralized anti-Vichy forces.

Koutaba — A settlement in the Bamounland, Noun Division, West Region. Also a major military and air base in Cameroon,

Kumba	The largest city in the Southwest Region and capital of Meme Division. It is located about 70 miles north of Limbe.
KNDP (Cameroon National Democratic Party)	Nationalist party in British Cameroons. It led the campaign that realized the reunification of British Southern Cameroons with former French Cameroun.
Limbe	Former Victoria. It is the capital of Fako Division in the Southwest Region.
Littoral	Coastal province of Cameroon. It consists of four divisions.
Loum	An agricultural town in the Mungo Division, in the north of the Littoral Region.
Maguida (Magida)	Name erroneously used for the peoples of the Moslem North that originated from the third group of Fulanis—the Fulanin Gida, comprising the fully sedentary Fulani communities.

Mamfe	The capital of Manyu Division in the Southwest Region.
Manjibo	A Bamoun village in the Noun Division.
Mankon	Mankon is a Ngemba kingdom and part of the city of Bamenda.
Maroua	The capital of the Extreme North Region and Diamare Division.
Mayo Tsanaga	A division in the Extreme North Region of Cameroon.
Mayo Tsava	A division in the Extreme North Region of Cameroon.
Mbengwi	The capital of Momo Division in the Northwest Region.
Mboh	A Bantu-speaking people of the Mungo Division in the Littoral Region, with fringes of their homeland in the Southwest and Western provinces.
Mokolo	Capital of Mayo Tsanaga Division.
Molyko	A suburb of Buea in the Southwest

	Region.
Mora	The capital of Mayo Tsava Division.
Mutengene	A junction town to Limbe, Buea, and Tiko, in Fako Division, Southwest Region.
Nde	Formerly called Banganté Division. It is found in the West Region of Cameroon.
Ngaoundéré	Capital of the Vina Division and Adamawa Region.
Ngemba	The second most populous peoples of the semi-Bantu group. The Ngemba peoples are found in the northern half of the Cameroon Grassland (Western Highlands), mostly in the Mezam and Momo Divisions of the Northwest Region. The Ngemba people related dialects.
Ngembaland	The Southwestern part of the Northwest Region that is composed of several traditional kingdoms or fondoms speaking closely related dialects.

Nkongsamba	The capital of the Mungo Division of Cameroon. It is also the largest city in the area.
Nkwen	A traditional Ngemba kingdom and part of the city of Bamenda.
North Region	Central of the Grand North Regions. It comprises four divisions.
Northwest Region	A province from the former Federal unit of West Cameroon and the former territory of British Southern Cameroons. Peopled by semi-Bantu groups of Tikar, Ngemba and Chamba speakers. Their compatriots in the Southwest Region collectively call them 'Graffis'.
NUDP (National Union for Democracy and Progress) Called UNDP *(Union Nationale pour la Démocratie et le Progrès)* in French	A political party in Cameroon founded by Samuel Eboua, a former minister of the regime Ahmadou Ahidjo. Bello Bouba Maigari, a former prime minister of the Biya regime, usurped the leadership of the party and has been its president since 1992.
Nzui-Mantor	Banganté-Bamileké word for the panther or leopard.

OK (One Cameroon)	An offshoot of the UPC after it was also banned in British Cameroons.
Peul	A French term for Fulani borrowed from the Wolof language.
RDPC (Rassemblement Démocratique du Peuple Camerounais), Called CPDM (Cameroon People's Democratic Movement) in English	The party in power in Cameroon. CNU renamed in 1985.
SDF (Social Democratic Front) or *FSD (Front Social-Démocrate)* in French	The political party that is described as the opposition leader in Cameroon. The SDF is led since its inception on May 26, 1990, by John Fru Ndi.
Semi-Bantu	The unique and unrelated peoples in Africa, comprising the Bamileké, Bamoun, Tikar, Ngemba and Chamba peoples.
Sokolo	A suburb in Limbe, Southwest Region.

South Region	Cameroon's southern coastal province. It comprises the three divisions of Ntem, Ocean and Dja and Lobo.
Southwest Region	Southwestern coastal province of Cameroon. It has four divisions. Formerly a part of British Southern Cameroons and the federal unit of West Cameroon.
Tchollíré	The capital of Rey Bouba Division in the North Region.
Tiko	A coastal town in Fako Division in the Southwest Region.
Tonga	Bamileké settlement and kingdom in the Nde Division, West Region.
Tuareg	A Berber-speaking people of the Mazigh group inhabiting the central Sahara from Southern Algeria and Tripolitania in Libya, to the middle Niger and the northern borders of Nigeria. They moved to the interior of the Sahara Desert to escape the Arab invasion of North Africa in the 7th and 8th century.

UDC (Union Démocratique du Cameroun) or CDU (Cameroon Democratic Union) in English — A political party in Cameroon founded by Adamou Ndam Njoya, former minister of the Ahmadou Ahidjo regime.

UNC (Union Nationale du Cameroun). Called CNU (Cameroon National Union) in English — Party formed in 1966 from the merger of political parties operating in Cameroon. It was headed by the first Cameroonian president Ahmadou Ahidjo.

UNDP (Union Nationale pour la Démocratie et le Progrès) or National Union for Democracy and Progress (NUDP) in English — A political party in Cameroon founded by Samuel Eboua, former minister of the regime Ahmadou Ahidjo. Bello Bouba Maigari, a former prime minister of the Biya regime, usurped the leadership of the party and has been its president since 1992.

UPC (Union of the Populations of the Cameroons) — First national and nationalistic party in Cameroon. The historic UPC was formed in 1948. Banned in 1955, it resorted to an armed struggle that continued well into the late 1960s.

Victoria — Former name of Limbe. Was founded

	in 1857 by missionaries for the settlement of rescued or freed slaves.
West Region	The southern half of the Western Highlands of Cameroon. It is populated by the Bamileké and Bamoun peoples. It is also Cameroon's cultural and agricultural heartland, and is remembered for its historic role as the center of the country's nationalism and liberation struggle against the French Army in the land. It comprises the six divisions of Bamboutous, Menoua, Mifi, Nde, Noun, and Upper Nkam.
Wolowose	Cameroonian word for a whore.
Wum	The capital of Menchum Division in the Northwest Region.
Yaoundé	Cameroon's second largest city and national capital. Also the capital of the Center Region and Nfoundi Division.

www.ingramcontent.com/pod-product-compliance
Lightning Source LLC
Chambersburg PA
CBHW031409250726
48656CB00002B/599